American Fishermen

American Fishermen

By ALBERT COOK CHURCH

With Text by JAMES B. CONNOLLY

New York · BONANZA BOOKS · *New York*

Contents

List of Illustrations

7

List of Illustrations

5. COD, HADDOCK, AND HALIBUT

6. SWORDFISHING OFF NANTUCKET

American Fishermen

1. *American Fishing*

AMERICAN fishing dates back to the early colonial days, though not as an industry except in the port of Gloucester.

The explorer *Champlain* sailed into Gloucester harbor in 1606, stayed there several weeks, and came back to France with great stories of the abundance of fish to be caught off Gloucester harbor and the rocky coast to the eastward. In the sixteen-thirties the Reverend Francis Higginson of the Boston settlement was writing to the folks back home of the succulence and lusciousness and plenitude of fish to be caught off the Cape Ann shore.

Gloucester was settled in 1623. Men began fishing there from the beginning; and so, Albert Cook Church, great marine photographer, properly opens his book with an illustration of a model of the sort of craft in which those early Gloucestermen went to sea. We scan the photograph of that Chebacco boat, and we cannot help thinking that the early fishing was as much an adventure as an industry. But an industry it was and has been since—with the adventure to be taken as part of the day's work, incidental always to a way of making a man's living.

Those early American fishing craft were no more than open boats with a little cuddy forward where a man might tuck in from the rain. In time the cuddy was enlarged, room was made for a couple of bunks and a fireplace with a brick or wooden chimney plastered over. The old-timers would smoke the less marketable fish in the chimney; and on Sunday, a day of rest always, they treated themselves to pancakes baked in the brick or plastered oven. Those old-time Gloucestermen were a God-fearing lot who never fished on Sunday; and clear up to the end of the last century many a Gloucester skipper would not allow Sunday fishing aboard his vessel.

Those early Gloucestermen would set out in those Chebacco boats

17

to be gone four or five days, sometimes a week. For rations they would have fried bread, corn meal, salt beef, and a jug of rum. In New England's colonial days, rum was always a staple article of commerce, and always a heartening drink to a man drenched by the rain or flying spray out to sea.

The early Gloucestermen fished off Cape Ann and along the Maine coast. Gradually they worked to the eastward and offshore, but not in the little Chebaccos. Bigger boats—ketches and pinkeys—came into use then.

For a long time, Gloucestermen held to the alongshore summer fishing only. That could not last, of course; men had to make a living all the year round; and so in time they went in for winter fishing, and ventured farther and farther to the eastward, to beyond Cape Sable and, eventually, to the great fishing shoals of the Grand Banks. The ketches and pinkeys may look comical now, with their high poops fore and aft, and their small square sails; but they were seagoing ladies of degree, good seaboats all, and big enough for seventeenth and eighteenth century uses. The pinkeys especially won a great name for themselves, serving as merchant ships of commerce to the far ports, and as privateersmen in 1776 and 1812.

The pinkeys gave way to the bigger, and even more weatherly, schooner type of sailing craft. They had to be weatherly if crews of men were to survive the winter fishing on the offshore banks. The shoals of the Grand Banks weren't the worst. Georges Bank was the terrible place in wintertime. Think of a fleet of vessels being anchored on Georges and one third of the fleet—14 vessels and 140 men—being lost in a single night! And tough night after tough night is the record of Georges Bank. The great losses there were caused by vessels being caught at anchor with the wicked shoals under their lee when the great gales roared down on them. Fishermen themselves will have it that given open water and their able vessels under sail, not all the gales that ever blew would be too much for them. That was in a later day, of course, when the superb schooners of the New England fleets were the wonder of the maritime world.

Albert Church has known these great schooners at firsthand, and more than knowing them firsthand, he knows how to appraise them for what they were—the fastest and most weatherly fore-and-aft rigged vessels of all time.

To their crews those great schooners were pleasure and business together. No yachtsmen, even yachtsmen racing for the America's Cup, ever got more joy from outsailing a foreign rival for an international cup than these fishermen got out of making the market before a rival after a hard passage from an offshore fishing bank.

Those great vessels were the outcome of the need to meet the heaviest winter seas and wind, and to make a fast passage to market after a good haul of fish. Early to market meant top prices; but there was pride of vessel also. Fishing captains and crews bragged far more of their fast able vessels after outsailing a rival than of their big share of money after making the top of the market.

As far back as the eighties, Burgess of Boston, victorious defender of the America's Cup, was designing Gloucester and Boston fishing schooners. Later leading designers—McManus, Lawlor, Crownshield, the younger Burgess, Paine—designed fishing schooners for Gloucester, Boston, and Provincetown captains. Fishing captains called for Cup Race yacht plans, and had vessels built to the Cup Race yacht lines; but they saw to it that tough three-inch oak and hard straight-grained pine went into their hulls, and stout spars and heavy gear above decks—no market basket hulls for them, or rigging that couldn't stand up before as much as a thirty-mile breeze. Racing was a joy always, but the fishing was also their bread and butter, life and death; and what good was a vessel that wouldn't bring them safely through a combination of the heaviest offshore gales of wind and high running seas?

They were beautiful and able, those vessels. And for seaworthiness? In 1892, Gloucester had an anniversary Fishermen's Race. The wind blew sixty miles an hour (official weather report) and Gloucester captains sailed out for that race with every sail set and the pledge that no sail would come off "except what the Lord took off!" The Lord took off plenty that day. The *Harry Belden* carried her whole four lower and both topsails through the rough going of that race. It was an untutored Gloucester fisherman standing by the finish line who roared to the gale that day: "The *Harry Belden* wins! The able *Harry Belden*, sailin' across the line on her side and her crew sittin' out on the keel!"

Albert Church gives space to quite a few of those fishing schooners. They rate the space, as do their captains and crews. Greatest of their kind were the schooners, and skillfully and daringly handled; and so the incredible tales—incredible to folk who never knew them—of their sail-carrying doings. The *Belden,* 110 feet overall, once sailed eighteen miles (sea miles always in this chronicle) in one hour and ten minutes. She once made the passage from clear of the north shoal of Georges to the Boston Lightship (154 miles) in ten hours flat.

The sail-carrying skippers were great ones for giving the vessel all the credit. The *Belden's* captain, Maurice Whalen, being asked if he found it rough going in the Anniversary Race, answered: "It was a bit choppy, but you know the *Belden*—she likes it choppy." She was rolling to her main swifters in that race. In case you don't know, the main swifters of the *Belden* were six feet above her quarter-deck.

Captain Tommie Bohlen, in the *Nannie Bohlen,* 117 feet overall, once sailed from Cape Sable to Gloucester in 14 hours, 25 minutes, an average of 15.6 knots. On hearing it said that his vessel must have had all the wind she could stand on that Cape Sable passage, Bohlen replied earnestly: "No, no! Not the *Bohlen!* She could've stood a little more!" It was Bohlen who once said: "I druv her and I druv her and I druv her! But could I make her quit? The man never lived who could make the *Nannie Bohlen* quit!"

In this unrivaled collection of fishing photographs, Albert Church gives us the successors to the *Belden* and the *Bohlen;* vessels that were perhaps faster than those great ones of the nineties, but not more able —no vessels could be that—and faster because bigger. Church gives us the *Gertrude Thebaud.* Racing the Canadian *Bluenose* in an International Fishermen's Race one year, the *Thebaud* sailed one leg of the course at a 15.6 knot clip, and kept a dry rail doing it. Captain Ben Pine rated the *Thebaud* as a 16½-knot vessel in a strong breeze of wind. Captain Pine, racing master also of the *Columbia,* rated her as a knot faster than the *Thebaud.* This writer was aboard the *Columbia* one time when she logged from 13½ to 14¼ knots for nine hours on end, and did it without once wetting her lee rail. I was on her one night the dry squalls were coming at her off Chebucto Head, and Captain Pine letting her take them with all sail set—when she must have been logging better than 17 knots. My guess, of course.

The *Columbia* was the most beautiful schooner I ever saw. When she would be tied up to her wharf in Gloucester, I was one of the crowd who used to stand on the stringpiece and gloat on the lines of her. She was beautiful! And to see her under sail and coming bow on in a smooth sea and a fresh breeze—to see her so, viewing her from under her lee bow, and the way she had of easing that bow in and out of the sea— well, the beautiful lady was Poetry herself then.

The *Henry Ford* is here, Clayton Morrissey, master, one of the great salt bankers out of Gloucester; the "long-sparred Clayt"—he was six feet four—who always chafed at racing his vessel over a short fifty-mile in-shore race course, who believed a vessel should be tested in a ten- or twelve-hundred mile drive from the offshore banks, who once stood lashed to the wheel for fourteen hours on a winter passage, and he to his waist in solid water throughout the whole fourteen hours.

The schooner *Mayflower* of the Boston fleet is here, the vessel that so decisively outsailed every vessel she hooked up with during her first summer on the Grand Banks that the Canadian Committee barred her from the International contest. They gave as their reason that she was built for a yacht and not a fisherman; a silly reason, because the fast Boston fishing schooners of that day were regularly outsailing the schooner yachts of anywhere near their tonnage. The *Mayflower* was built to go fishing, and for eighteen years, winter and summer, she went fishing out of Boston. To revenge herself on the *Bluenose,* the *Mayflower* went over the race course that first year, and her manner of outsailing the *Bluenose* was scandalous to view.

There is a photograph here of the schooner *Elsie* and her racing sailing master of that day—skillful, sail-carrying, modest Martie Welch. He had previously taken the fourteen-year-old *Esperanto* fresh from three months of salt fishing on the Grand Banks, and with no recutting of her wind-blown, ill-fitting sails—there wasn't time for it—had won the First International Fishermen's Race.

Offshore banks fishermen do love their vessels. Captain Alden Geele, salt bank skipper and owner of the *Elsie,* was the Clayt Morrissey type.

He stood on the deck of the press boat and watched *Elsie* racing the *Bluenose*. The *Bluenose* was 21 feet longer, 2 feet wider, 2 feet deeper, and spread 2,000 more square feet of canvas than the *Elsie;* yet for 28 miles the great little *Elsie* led the big *Bluenose* in her first race, and Alden Geele's pride of vessel was something to see. But when the big fellow passed her later in the race, I stood beside Captain Geele, the tough old salt banker who had battled through forty years of Grand Banks fishing. Gales o' wind? Huh! But this day he watched his little *Elsie* take a beating, and: "My little *Elsie!* My poor little *Elsie!*" he was saying over and over.

We get a line on the danger of the offshore fishing from the record of what happened to most of those Race Cup schooners. The pity of it, and yet the almost inevitable ending. Speaking only of the race con-tenders and the two other vessels named here: The *Belden*, the *Bohlen*, the *Henry Ford, Esperanto, Elizabeth Howard, Progress, Puritan*, the *Elsie*, and the *Columbia* were lost. Alden Geele's little *Elsie* and the beautiful *Columbia* went down with all hands.

Church's photographs give us almost a course in wooden shipbuild-ing. He starts off with that famous old Essex shipyard horse hauling the timber to the stocks, and carries us on through the launching of the completed hull and her being towed to her home port, usually Glouces-ter or Boston, to be rigged and fitted out. He gives us the water-front loungers, inspecting the new arrival. And what a scalding she will get if she lacks a single item of the qualities that go to make a fast and able fisherman!

Since away back yonder, New England home yards, Maine and Mas-sachusetts largely, have been building most of our wooden ships. From New England forests came the tall, straight-grained pine logs for the spars, the tough oak for the planking of the deep water and coasting fleets—the clipper ships for the foreign commerce, the privateersmen and regular man o'wars men, the offshore fishing fleets. The Cape Ann yards built most of the Gloucester and Boston fishing craft, and Essex was the great Cape Ann yard.

More than three centuries ago Essex was building fishing vessels. She is still building them. It was, and is, wooden hulls always. For a long

time Essex builders had only to step out of doors to find all the fine
timber they needed. In time they denuded the Cape Ann country of
timber. Particular people, those Essex craftsmen. There was the matter
of masts, now. In later years they went far from home, even to Georgia
and Oregon for suitable spar timber.

A Gloucester skipper, Alec Griffin, had his doubts one time of the
soundness of his new imported masts. He was off the Nova Scotia shore,
on his way to the Grand Banks, when he ran head on into a northeast
winter gale. "A good chance right here," said Captain Alec, "to find out
about those new sticks of mine." He hauled his vessel up by the wind,
and drove her with all sails set, first on one tack and then on the other,
for fifty hours in a living gale. Well, his new spars were still up there.
"They must be all right, at that," said Alec.

Masts had to be sound to withstand the tremendous pressure of strong
winds against the big sails. It's no good luck for a vessel with weak spars
to be caught with shoals to leeward and a gale of wind blowing. And the
hulls had better be strongly framed and strongly planked and properly
treenailed. That treenailing—trunneling—is always important. Nothing
like wooden treenails to hold planks to the frames. Metal nails will work
loose; but you take wooden nails, an inch or thereabouts in diameter,
let them fit snugly when driven in, and you have something to stand by a
vessel. The water swells them up, makes them fit all the tighter. I was
with a Gloucester skipper, George Peeples, one time in a great gale in
ten fathoms of water on Georges South Shoal. Under twenty fathoms
of water in bad weather on Georges is something to prepare against.
We were in a little vessel, the *Lafayette*—46 feet on the water line—and
we were in ten fathoms. I watched the short high seas roaring down on
our little hull, and I took to wondering how long she would stand the
pounding before coming apart. Peeples made me feel better when he
said: "She'll hold together. I looked to her building on John Chisholm's
wharf in Gloucester. I drove every trunnel in her myself."

More two-masted schooners have been built in Essex than in any one
place in the world. And there is where the expert craftsmen live. Expert
and conscientious. The lives of crews of men will be depending on their
workmanship, so there must be no scamping. They could be trusted, but

by way of no harm it was the habit of fishing captains with a new vessel building to spend most of their time ashore between trips in the Essex yards watching how their new one was coming on.

The sparmakers, too—usually in Gloucester they would be—are great craftsmen. To see them take a long pine stick and begin to shape it! With no more than a string, a piece of chalk, a maul, two or three tools, and their eyes—don't forget their eyes—they would start in. It would all be done by hand. And then to see them on the last day—the space about them ankle deep in pine chips—squinting at the long spar from one end, then from the other end, then from each side. And then straight down a few times, and then do it all over again, with the adz, maybe, taking off another shaving of the thickness and square area of a baby's thumbnail. And then a final, loving pat, and to the owner or vessel captain it was meant for: "There she is. Varnish her and step her—there she is!"

Craftsmen all, those shipbuilding craftsmen of old Cape Ann.

Spring in Gloucester means mackerel catchers get ready. And what goes on in Gloucester goes on in other fishing ports along the North Atlantic coast. Sails are taken down from lofts and bent on masts, seines are overhauled and freshly tarred, vessels are put up on the railway and scrubbed and painted. Then it is Southward Ho! to meet the north-bound mackerel.

Mackerel are a puzzle to fishermen. Just where they come from in the spring and just where they go to in the fall they do not know. Along in March, steamer captains from southern ports begin to report seeing them to the south'ard, sometimes as far south as the Florida coast, but more usually off Cape Hatteras. The seiners (mackerel catchers) aim to pick them up off the Virginia Capes and stay with them while they make their way along the coast to the Gulf of St. Lawrence in the fall and back off to the south New England coast and away from the sight of fishermen till spring comes again.

Gloucestermen speak of mackerel catching as a gentleman's life. No heaving and hauling of heavy trawling gear and rowing a little dory through breaking seas; and that in winter, too. Nothing like that. Mackerel crews stand their trick at the wheel and their lookout watch on the foremast head, and dress or salt the fish when they get them; but that is light work compared to what the trawlers have to do.

Fish are sighted by the lookouts aloft. "School-O!" they cry, and down from the masthead come the lookouts, sometimes by a backstay to save time. Into the big seine boat and the little dory they pile, two men in the dory and fourteen men in the seine boat. The skipper will be standing in the stern of the 38- or 40-foot seine boat with a long steering oar; the seine heaver, the strong man of the crew, will be tossing the seine in great armfuls over the side; the dozen men at the oars will be driving the boat toward the oncoming school of mackerel. Let two or three seine boats be heading for the same school, and then there is a real boat race; and sometimes a riot at the end of the race.

Mackerel are surface fish, and they travel in schools. Lookouts spot them miles away by what looks like a tide rip, sometimes like a wind rip, on the surface of the sea. That seine boat will be aiming to head off the school and lay a net of twine a quarter mile long and twenty fathoms deep around the oncoming fish. Once around the school, the dory and seine boat together purse in the bottom of the seine; and there is that school of mackerel tucked away. Then the cook, the only man left aboard the vessel, brings the vessel alongside. The crew bail the fish aboard with dip nets that will hoist aboard a barrel or more of fish with every dip.

In the all-sail days, if a market port be handy, the haul of any size, and the wind fair, the fish would be iced and the vessel driven to market; if not, the fish would be dressed and salted and stowed below till enough of them were there to make a run to market worth while. In those days, rival skippers getting a haul of mackerel at the same time would make a great race of it to the nearest market port. I was on a Savannah steamer bound for New York one time when the Gloucester schooner *Constellation* came swinging in from out of the offshore morning mists. She was New York bound also. It was spring and there was sure to be a great price for the new mackerel, and somewhere in the mists was maybe another seiner or two bound for New York. A fair fresh breeze was blowing and the little schooner—little compared to our steamer— was swinging every light and heavy sail she had. We were doing better than thirteen knots on the steamer, and from dawn till dark of that day, for two hundred miles along the Jersey coast, that little schooner stayed abreast of us, with our passengers lining our rail and cheering her all the way. Her skipper, Thad Morgan, spent most of that day standing in her lee gangway, his boots filled with water, and driving his vessel to a faster pace with a steady forward motion of his arms.

In the old days it was all daylight fishing, but with the later and harder driving captains, night fishing came into vogue. On dark moonless nights, lookouts aloft spot mackerel by the phosphorescent trail they leave on the sea. It is like white fire. On such nights the seine boat and the dory men will be towing astern of the vessel to a short painter. The vessel will be close hauled, and if the sea be choppy and the vessel doing eleven or twelve knots close hauled, the men in the seine boat and dory are in for a lively evening. Or a whole night of it maybe, those seiners being great ones for sticking to it while a hope of fish is before them.

Along in June reports begin to come of swordfish showing off the Jersey and Block Island shores.

The swordfishermen are already fitting out. Half a dozen dories and as many barrel buoys, a few hundred fathoms of buoy line, a hat full of lily irons (harpoons), a hold full of ice, and there's a crew of swordfishermen ready to put to sea.

There will of course be the vessel, smaller always than the seiners or trawlers. The vessel will have planks lashed across her fore topmast for the lookouts; and there will be a pulpit—a small platform at the end of the bowsprit for the striker, who is the harpooner. A waist-high iron rail to the front and sides of the platform will be rigged to hold the striker safe aboard when he lunges forward to drive the harpoon home.

Smart lookouts aloft are important, but the great fellow aboard a swordfisherman is the striker. Wary fish these, fast-moving fish: even when the lookouts pilot the vessel close aboard a fish, the striker has to hit instantly, and he has to hit hard. Swordfish come as thick through as a 42-gallon barrel; and they are all solid meat, which means that a strong arm is needed to drive an iron through them.

Also—what with the vessel and the fish being both in motion and usually not heading in the same direction—a striker needs to have a good eye. Captain George Peeples of Gloucester had the name among his crew of harpooning 197 swordfish without a miss.

Swordfishing appeals to amateur sportsmen, and it is great fun to rig a power yacht with a pulpit and go after them in smooth water; but the men who make a living at it find the game goes rough at times. A striker will be in the pulpit when a heavy ground swell sets in. The vessel will plunge her pulpit under and the striker will go to his knees in solid water. He will pay no attention. Soon he will be going in to his waist. Well, no harm in that. Not long perhaps before he will be going in to his ears. After that has happened a dozen times or so he will come back inboard, but not because he was getting wet. I was with George Peeples one time after he had plunged in to his ears and came inboard. "The hell of shoal water and a swell on," explained George mournfully, "is the sea rolling up and going a dirty color so a man can't see the fish, and a man can't strike what he can't see, so he might's well come in and give the lookouts aloft a rest."

Swordfish like to play around in the shoal water of the fishing banks off the New England coast. To illustrate the danger in shoal water—this from personal observation—ten swordfishing craft were between the Nantucket lightship and Georges South Shoal that day of the great summer gale of July 28, 1911. The wind blew eighty miles an hour for four hours, then hauled and blew a hundred miles an hour from the opposite direction. Four or five of the fleet that hadn't run early had to lay there and take it. And laying there and watching the short masthead-high seas come rolling down at them, they were hoping that no specially wicked one would roll them so far down that they would not be able to roll back again. We were all small vessels. The *Lafayette's* sister ship, the *Nokomis*, 46 feet water line, wasn't able to roll back. She lay not far from us, but the seas were too high and steep pitched for us to see over them to her. We only knew she was gone when we picked up her wreckage next day.

On the front page of the New York Sunday *Sun* of July 30 later, we read of the bodies of four being picked up off Nantucket. On the same front page we read of a 700-foot ocean liner that was so bounced around during the gale that they had to give up a prayer meeting that some of the passengers had called for. Our fellows read of the *Nokomis* tragedy with grave faces—the same thing might have happened to our little one; but the talk of a 700-foot ship being bounced around—they thought that was comical.

All fishing craft today are auxiliary or all-power boats. Up to the year 1900, American fishing craft were practically all-sail. In that year, Gloucester launched her first auxiliary schooner. A few years later she was launching an all-power steamer. In the year 1900, fifty all-sail halibut catchers were sailing out of Gloucester. In the present year, 1940, there are just two of those fifty halibut catchers left. And that is the story all along the line. In those forty years, American Gloucester all-sail fleet is gone. The all-power vessels in the American fishing are here to stay. A good thing that the perilous and terrifically hard way of the old days is gone; yet whoever has known what great men that old all-sail life developed must almost regret the passing of it.

Folk reading of the deeds of the fishermen of the all-sail days have wondered what part of them were true and what part fiction. Let one who knew them say here that the fiction never exceeded the tall reality. The vessels, and the captains who sailed them in their hair-raising passages, were unequaled; and the crew men too were great.

Take the men who left the vessel regularly to heave and haul their heavy trawls and row their little dories in the weather of the offshore banks in wintertime; who so frequently went astray in fog and snow and bitter cold, and stayed astray for days and sometimes lived; who made themselves live by reason of their amazing stamina and stark manhood.

Take the fresh halibuter, Howard Blackburn, who went astray with his dory mate from Captain Alec Griffin's vessel, the *Grace L. Fearing*, one February on the Grand Banks. A bitter cold northwest wind was blowing, and there was a thick snow; and soon high running seas were tossing their little dory about. It grew colder. On the third night Howard's dory mate froze to death. Howard could feel himself freezing. His fingers were going white and stiff on him. He looked at them, and knowing that if they froze straight and stiff he wouldn't be able to hold the oars and keep on rowing and make the land, he curled his fingers around the handles of the oars so that they would freeze in shape for him to keep on rowing. And his fingers froze in that shape and he kept on rowing, and after five days and nights he made land. He lost all his fingers, both thumbs, and part of each foot. He was crippled for life after it; but he made land with the body of his dead dory mate. And there, I submit, was a full-sized man.

Dory fishing on the offshore banks is pretty nearly done away with. Men stay on the decks of their power boats nowadays, lower a big bag overboard, let it drag the bottom, and scoop in any loose fish along the road. The crews warp the big bag aboard after two or three hours of dragging, empty the bag, lower it back overboard, dress and stow the fish, stand their turn at the wheel.

It is no wheel on an open deck, nor the helmsman lashed to keep him from being washed overboard by the big seas breaking aboard. No! And no wearing a woolen mask over the face to keep a man's face from freezing with the winter blast spilling off the big mainsail. No! It is a safe wheelhouse, sometimes steam-heated, for the helmsman nowadays.

"Well, that's all right, why not a bit of comfort?" say the old-timers, even while shaking their heads at some of the new inventions. One day last month an oldster was watching a new big-power dragger warp into the pier. "Is it true," he asked, "that she has shower baths for men coming off watch? Yes? Shower baths! Cripes! And the times we wouldn't get out of our wet clothes for a fortnight it might be. And turn in to our bunks for a week at a time, maybe, with our clothes still wet. Ah, man, but fishing is all comfort these times."

It is more comfortable, but it is still a hard and a dangerous life at times. The offshore banks can still go pretty rough, what with their gales of wind and masthead-high seas, especially in the wintertime. Take a peek at Church's photo of that ice-cased dragger just in from a winter passage from Georges. Surely a few high seas broke aboard her along the road.

Fishermen rarely go introspective over the dangers they have passed; and a fine habit, a good protective device say. Forgetting dangers passed saves much wear and tear on the nervous system; which forgetfulness is conducive to added years of life. But they do go thoughtful at times, like the famous Jack Mason, the Gloucester fresh halibuter. Jack's dory was capsized in heavy weather, his dory mate was washed off the dory bottom and lost. After six hours of rough riding on the bottom of the dory, Jack was picked up. Being asked if he thought he was gone any time, and what he was thinking of when he thought he was gone, he replied: "You know it was April, springtime, and I thought it was damned tough to go fishin' all winter and be lost in the spring."

The marine photographs of Albert Church deserve more than a casual line of praise. The photographs herein were not made in the peace and quiet of a studio ashore. Fishermen out to sea do not knock off work and stand around and pose for pictures. A man doing pictures of them has to go after them; and there are times when that means risking danger.

Off Gloucester harbor some years ago I took in a Fishermen's Elimination Race with Albert Church. We were placed aboard the starting boat, an American destroyer, and she was anchored at the windward end of the starting line. With less than a minute to go, half a dozen big schooners headed for the starting line, and the skipper of each vessel was meaning to secure the windward berth.

The *Elizabeth Howard*, Captain Ben Pine, was to windward. Two vessels were crowding her closely for the windward berth. The *Howard* held on, even when it looked as if she could not possibly squeeze between the next vessel and our destroyer. The *Howard* was a big schooner, 128 feet long, and she had 110 tons of ballast in her hold. She came head on for us at ten knots. If ever she hit the destroyer head on, she would cut right through her, send her to the bottom right there, and a boiler or two would likely go up as the ship went down.

No pleasant prospect! "She's coming straight for our midship! Beat it, everybody!" yelled Captain Charlie Harty. There was a stampede of Gloucester skippers, bluejackets, officials, newsmen, and invited guests for the fore and after ends of the ship.

Ben Pine was too busy at the wheel to do anything about it; but Alec Chisholm, young Gloucester businessman, volunteer member of the *Howard's* crew, and a smart hand aboard a vessel, leaped aft and let the main sheet go by the run. The end of the *Howard's* bowsprit was then all but touching the destroyer's side. The wind spilled out of the main sail, the big headsails filled and swung the *Howard* off. The end of the

Howard's bowsprit scraped the paint off the destroyer's side for 150 feet.

"Wheeyew!" murmured Charlie Harty, "close enough!" And led the way from his end of the ship to amidship. Here was Albert Church sliding another plate into the after end of his camera. "Got two," said Albert. "The first one of her coming straight at us bow on ought to be a swell shot." Albert had stayed right there through it all.

Albert Church is a great marine photographer. He is also an artist. I was with him some years ago on an America's Cup Race occasion off Newport. That was the year he chartered a dirigible balloon to shoot the racing yachts from the air. He paid the money in advance. When the race day came it was all low clouds and no pictures. The hire of the dirigible left Albert bankrupt of cash, which he did not mind. But not getting the race boats from the air—that was tough luck for an original idea.

Albert Church is an artist, but has to take his marine pictures when and where he can get them. Even so, he manages an artistic one every now and then. There are some herein.

James B. Connolly

Brookline, Mass.
September 30, 1940

2. *From Pinkey to Clipper Fishermen*

1. *Columbia,* of Gloucester. The schooner *Columbia,* designed by W. Starling Burgess and built by Arthur Story at Essex, Mass., is generally considered to have been the fastest fisherman out of Gloucester.

2. Model of Dogbody square stern Chebacco boat, 1780–1800. From the Smithsonian Institution collection.

3. Model of the New England Fishing Pinkey *Porpoise*, of Gloucester. This model is authentic of the period 1810–30, and is included in the collection of the Smithsonian Institution.

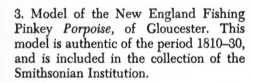

4. Model of early-type fishing schooner, period 1820. From the collection of the Peabody Museum, Salem, Mass.

5. The *Maine,* last of the old pinkeys, arrives at Gloucester, 1910.

6. A quartering view of the old pinkey. This view shows to good advantage how the sheer was gracefully raised aft to the peak of the stern, called the "pink," from which the type derived its name.

7. The *Maine,* laying at the dock, Vincent Cove, Gloucester.

8. The wooden traveler, pinkey *Maine.* The links of the old-fashioned anchor chain are of special interest, being of a type obsolete for many years.

9. Quarter-deck, pinkey *Maine.* This shows the traveling tiller, arrangement of wheel ropes and the transom post, cut out to receive the end of the main boom as a boom crutch.

10. The last of an old-timer. The *Eastern Light,* a 70-ton vessel built at Kennebunk, Maine, in 1866, then skippered by David Lane, was owned by the old Gloucester firm of Maddocks & Company. She was the last vessel afloat of her type, and went to pieces where she sank, at East Gloucester, some years ago. The old-fashioned wooden traveler can be seen just aft the windlass.

11. Low tide, Harbor Cove, Gloucester.

12. The *Helen B. Thomas*, of Boston, was the first knockabout type fisherman.

13. Between 1910–20 splendid vessels of this type were built, the last of the sail-driven fishermen.

14. *Columbia* reeling off 14½ knots.

15. Gloucester fisherman *Elizabeth Howard,* white ghost of the fishing banks.

16. *Bluenose*, Canadian champion of the North Atlantic.

17. The *Henry Ford* shaves close to the outer mark.

18. Schooner *Elsie* of Gloucester.

19. Gloucester schooner *Gertrude L. Thebaud* in racing trim.

20. The *Yankee,* a smart fisherman from the Boston fleet.

21. The mastheadman, schooner *Thebaud.*

22. Bow section view of the *Henry Ford*.

23. Polishing up the *Bluenose*. Comparison between the bow section views of *Bluenose* and the *Henry Ford* is interesting. While hauled out at Gloucester for measurement and repainting before the race, every bit of the underbody was scrubbed and smoothed down to give the speedy vessel every chance to do her best.

24. The *Ford* hauls out. Preparations for the fishermen's race off Gloucester always arouse great enthusiasm, and visitors from all points of the compass arrive to see these famous craft when hauled out on the railway. The *Ford's* clean run and splendid bearing under the quarters are coming in for admiring attention from the fishermen standing by.

25. *Thebaud* racing off Halifax in a tumbling sea.

26. The *Thebaud* racing down the wind off Halifax, Nova Scotia.

27. Tuning up for the race. Clayton Morrissey puts the *Henry Ford* through her paces before tackling the slippery *Howard.*

28. *Columbia* begins to work out a lead on the speedy *Ford*.

29. Fore topmast carried away! All hands scramble lively to take in the fisherman's staysail trailing to leeward as the fore topmast goes by the board.

30. *Elizabeth Howard* and *Shamrock* before the wind.

31. The "scandalized" staysail. When fishermen set a sail upside down they call it scandalized. Here we see the *Henry Ford* running off the wind with the staysail inverted, set as a spinnaker.

32. Captain Clayton Morrissey of Gloucester, skipper of *Henry Ford*.

33. The *Henry Ford* becalmed, a half mile from the finish.

34. Tom McManus, of Boston (center), famous designer of fishermen, looks the *Bluenose* over as she hauls out before the race at Gloucester.

35. *Bluenose* on the ways at Gloucester.

36. Measuring the *Bluenose* at Halifax. Roue, designer of *Bluenose*, watches the official measurer with interest as he checks the floating batten to determine the water-line measurement.

37. *Bluenose* returns from a tuning-up trial spin before the race.

38. Flattening sheets for a drive to windward, *Bluenose*.

39. The weather bow, *Bluenose*.

40. *Bluenose* finishes astern the *Thebaud* at Gloucester.

41. *Bluenose* flies her colors to welcome *Columbia* to Halifax.

42. A famous Gloucester skipper. Marty Welch, famous skipper of the *Esperanto*, *Elsie*, *Lucania*, *Helena*, and other Gloucester craft, here surveys the *Elsie* from the quarter-deck by the wheel as the vessel prepares to leave for Halifax to race the Canadian schooner *Bluenose* for the International Fishermen's Trophy.

43. *Bluenose* picks up a breeze on a silvery sea.

44. Finding the trim of the *Thebaud*. Skipper Ben Pine of Gloucester, to windward, takes a look around and sizes up the trim of the headsail.

45. Decks awash, schooner *Gertrude L. Thebaud*.

46. *Thebaud* rolls the sea to leeward as she stretches out for a trial spin offshore.

47. The Fishermen's Race. Schooner *Gertrude L. Thebaud* leading *Bluenose* off Gloucester.

48. *Bluenose,* to windward, slides out past the *Thebaud* at Halifax.

49. Close quarters. Things are always likely to happen during a fishermen's race, and it looked as though we might get hooked aloft about the time this shot was made. *Elsie's* main boom squeezed by the *Thebaud's* balloon stay by an inch or two and nothing else happened.

50. The *Henry Ford* blankets *Columbia* at the weather mark.

51. *Thebaud* pulls out from under the *Elsie's* lee.

52. *Thebaud* leads *Elsie* before the wind. The *Elsie*, carrying 600 square feet more canvas than allowed under the International Fishermen's Race rules, was still no match for the *Thebaud*.

53. The stern chase.

54. *Elsie* leads the *Thebaud* around the mark.

55. *Columbia* beats the *Ford* in a close race.

56. Running before the wind, wing and wing, *Bluenose* leads *Columbia* as they near the leeward mark off Halifax, crews standing by to trim sheets.

57. The *Ford* hits up a hot pace as she wets the lee rail.

58. A silhouette of the *Henry Ford*.

59. Bound for the fishermen's races. The knockabout fisherman *Louise Marshall,* stacking twenty dories, heads out from Eastern Point off Gloucester bound for the fishermen's race, a veritable floating grandstand.

60. *Bluenose* and *Henry Ford* start in light airs; the destroyer is acting as committee boat.

61. Close quarters at the start. *Thebaud* leads *Bluenose* across the starting line, the wind almost dead astern. *Bluenose*, as overtaking vessel, is having difficulty in keeping clear, her bowsprit having established an overlap, and with jumbo hauled to windward and foresail to starboard Walters endeavors to bear away to prevent fouling.

62. Carrying sail, *Thebaud* homeward bound.

63. Sheeting home the balloon.

64. *Columbia,* the gem of the ocean.

65. *Yankee*, a 115-foot schooner built at Essex in 1921, was a smart fisherman of the Boston fleet.

66. *Bluenose* races through the sunny sea.

67. *Bluenose* paints a picture on the North Atlantic.

68. A close start between *Bluenose* and the *Henry Ford*.

69. *Columbia* stretches her wings before the race.
70. Schooner *Shamrock* with Martin Welch at the wheel off Gloucester.

71. Schooner *Elizabeth Howard* traveled fast with started sheets.

72. *Shamrock* speeds along in the gathering breeze.

73. Sunlight and shadow.

74. The *Elizabeth Howard* crosses the path of the sun.

75. The *Elizabeth Howard* flirts with the morning sun.

76. The *Howard* running off the wind winged out.

77. The *Henry Ford* smashing through the sea.

78. The *Thebaud,* running wing and wing in failing airs.

79. Captain John Matheson of Gloucester, famous sail carrier and helmsman, at *Thebaud's* wheel.

80. Skipper Jim Fowler, Gloucester, former captain of the *Massasoit*.

81. The lee quarter, *Henry Ford*.

82. "By the wind, steady as you go, sir."

3. Building of the Gloucestermen

83. The old shipyards at Essex, Mass. For generations vessels for the fishery have been built in the quaint little village of Essex, Massachusetts, situated on an inland creek but few miles from Gloucester. Two of the yards are still in operation, those of the old Tarr & James firm and that of Arthur D. Story. James built the *Esperanto* and *Mayflower*, and Story the *Ford* and *Columbia*. The view shows the Story yards, with the *Henry Ford* nearing completion, at the right.

84. Timber for the new vessel. The faithful old horse, a familiar figure for many years at the James shipyard, wore a beaten path between the timber yard and bandsaw, with oak to be sawn into frames for a fisherman.

85. Setting up the frames. Four sets of the midship frames are here in position on a section of the keel, and framing will proceed fore and aft of these as other sections of the keel are scarfed in, and the frames lined up.

86. Fastening the stem piece in position. After boring up through the tough white oak, the bolts and fastenings are drifted in by sledge.

87. The same stem later, when fully planked in.

88. Vessel in frame, ribboned out, and planking begun. The frames set in position, lined up, and ribboned out fair with battens; planking the lower or garboard strakes has begun. The double frames, closely spaced together, are very heavy and rugged.

89. Vessel in frame, quartering view. The splendid, clean lines of this craft indicate she will be a big sailer, as they say in Gloucester, meaning she is bound to be a fast vessel.

91. Planking the garboard, driving treenails. Treenails, generally called "trunnels," are usually of locust, sledged in tightly after boring and oak wedges driven into both ends, making the strongest fastening known to shipwrights for securing planking.

92. Ceiling a vessel at Bishop's, looking aft. The heavy, three-inch yellow pine ceiling trunnels fastened fore and aft along the inside of such strong frames indicate this to be a first-class vessel, and everything must be the best.

93. Ceiling the hull inside, looking forward.

94. Yellow pine and white oak.

95. Shipwrights, Gloucester.

96. *Mayflower* planked up at James's, Essex.

97. Building *Mayflower*.

98. An able vessel building for the halibut fishery. Comparison with lines of *Mayflower* is interesting.

99. Deck closed in, aft to the cabin house.

100. Fitting the plank. The cabin structure will be built here. Two lower planks for the sides are already in position.

101 and 102. Each workman is experienced at a particular task. This mechanic, mitering the hatch coamings, is an expert, deeply interested in his task.

103. Looking forward on deck, from aft the sternpost. The substantial structure of this fine vessel is evident and the heavy oak timber of the sternpost, deck beams, and carlings indicate great strength.

104. Spiking down the deck planking.

105. Every detail of the construction is under the watchful eye of the foreman, for many years a master builder.

106. Knightheads and stanchions.

107. Planking the quarter-deck, showing heavily timbered stern and transom. The workmen, splendid examples of the type of men engaged in shipbuilding in New England yards, have been employed here for many years. The yard, however, is not now in operation, having been abandoned after the death of Mr. Bishop some years after the photo was taken, in 1910.

108. Deck structures rapidly taking shape.

109. Stem and sternpost of a fisherman hewed out. The white oak, stored away for years to season thoroughly, is hard as rock, so tough it is difficult to work.

110. Knockabout fisherman *Gladys and Nellie* ready to launch.

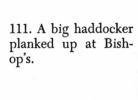

111. A big haddocker planked up at Bishop's.

112. The Burgess-designed *Mayflower*, flying greyhound of the sea, ready to launch. A glance at the slippery lines of this vessel reveals the fact she was fast. Built as a prospective contender for the International Fishermen's Trophy at Halifax, her challenge proved unacceptable, and she was never raced over a triangular course. As a consequence her relative speed compared to existing vessels was never decided.

113. Launching *Mayflower* from the James yard, Essex.

114. *Mayflower* under sail.

115. The powerful hull of *Columbia,* ready to launch at Story's.

116. *Columbia* splashes into the creek at Essex.

117. *Columbia.* The beautiful lines of this remarkable vessel are clearly apparent, and it is not surprising she proved to be the fastest fisherman out of Gloucester.

118. Launch of *Stiletto*.

119. After the launch at Bishop's. *Stiletto* was one of the last fine
vessels built at the John Bishop yard on Vincent's Cove, Gloucester,
in 1910. Without the weight of ballast and spars, to be added later,
the new vessel floats high above her water line.

120. The *Puritan*, of Gloucester. Another of the fine vessels among the later built craft at Essex was the *Puritan*, afterward lost on Sable Island. She greatly resembled *Columbia*.

121. *Mayflower* afloat after launch. As soon as afloat, the schooner is towed to Gloucester to take ballast aboard and step the spars. The tug alongside *Mayflower* is ready to go.

122. The *Henry Ford* has a narrow escape. Schooner *Henry Ford*, in tow bound for Gloucester after launching at Essex, broke adrift during a squall and went ashore on the sands of Wingershaek Beach, close to the rocks. She was afterward floated with little sign of damage. The photo gives an excellent view of deck arrangement aboard a fisherman.

123. The shipyard of John Bishop, Gloucester, 1909. Ready to launch, rudder braced to prevent damage as the heavy vessel races down the ways into the frozen waters of Vincent Cove, the splendid craft seems loath to leave the hands of the faithful shipwrights that built her.

124. The Gloucester-built steering gear. The patent steering gear, fitted in position, and the wheelbox will soon be completed. Cabin roof, skylight, windlass, hatchcovers, and details are about finished, ready to step the spars.

125. Sparmakers finishing up the masts of a big fisherman. The blacksmith has been busily engaged in forging the many bands, eyebolts, chain plates, and scores of iron fittings that go with the gear and equipment. Already galvanized, it is ready to fit in place.

126. Stepping the spars.

127 and 128. Rigging the *Mayflower*, T Wharf, Boston. After launch at Essex, schooner *Mayflower* of Boston towed to that port to complete rigging at T Wharf, where she attracted thousands of spectators to the water front.

129. Low tide, Gloucester. The new vessel, nearly ready for sea, awaits final touches of the riggers; slinging booms, bending sail, and the thousand and one details that necessarily attend completion and commissioning of an able fisherman.

130. Blocks, anchor chain, and trawl anchors.

131. Trial trip of schooner *Columbia*.

132. Trying out the new vessel. With started sheets and a good breeze she seems to be traveling along at a good clip, greatly enjoyed by crew and guests.

133. Ben Pine, racing skipper of *Columbia, Elizabeth Howard,* and *Gertrude L. Thebaud.*

134. **The ship that never sailed.** The old weatherbeaten buildings and the keel of a ship that never sailed were all that remained of the abandoned Lantz shipyard years ago, and they have now disappeared. Formerly both the Lantz and Oxner & Story yards built fishermen by the creek at Essex, but only the old Tarr & James and Arthur Story yards survive in 1940.

4. *The Mackerel Fishery*

135. "All hands, over she goes!" The 40-foot seineboat, weighing two tons, ten feet longer than the space between the fore and main rigging, goes out just the same, one end at a time, until swung clear by the tackles.

136. Gloucester harbor during the mackerel season. During the height of the mackerel season, the Gloucester water front presented a scene of great activity. Wharves were lined with vessels refitting after discharging fares of salt mackerel taken along the Nova Scotia Cape Shore, as the fleet prepared to cruise along the coast and run their fares fresh into T Wharf at Boston.

137. Twine for the seiners and gill netters. During winter the seine lofts repair damaged mackerel seines and gill nets, overhaul the gear, and make new twine, which is tarred and seasoned in the air during early spring, ready for the fleet fitting out.

138. Mackerel gill nets. Gill nets used by small craft called netters or drifters are set before nightfall and left afloat until morning during moonlight conditions when nets are less liable to fire in the water from phosphorescence. Mackerel swimming against the nets become entangled by the gills, and are removed when the nets are underrun at dawn.

139. A stitch in time saves nine. Old canvas is overhauled and repaired usually during the winter, but recutting and alterations are often required and sailmakers are busy before the fleet gets away.

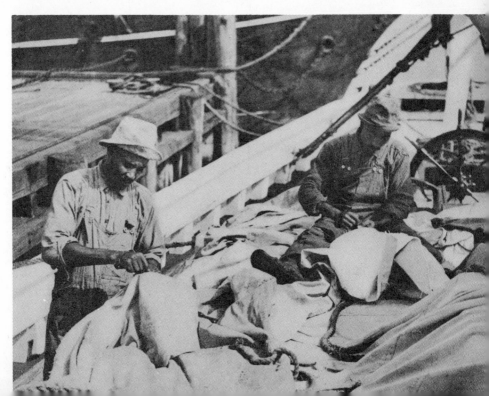

140. Seiners preparing for sea. The early spring months see great activity around the harbor at Gloucester, the wharves lined with lofty sparred vessels being groomed for the season. Hundreds of barrels of salt are heaped on the docks, ready to be loaded aboard the seiners before they leave for the Cape Shore trip, off the Nova Scotia coast.

141. The seineboats used in the mackerel fishery are a remarkably efficient type, built rugged for hard service, and are wonderful sea boats. They are carried on deck when making passage, and towed astern or from booms alongside when cruising on the grounds.

142. Icing up. Nowadays the custom is to fill ice pens below with machine-chopped ice through bunker plates in the deck, much less laborious than formerly.

143. Standing by, ready to sail. This photo was made aboard schooner *Alert*, of Gloucester, in 1906. Launched that spring, the vessel, high line in the seining fleet, was lost at Port-au-Port, Newfoundland, during a terrific storm in December the same year, while after a cargo of frozen herring.

144. An auxiliary seiner off for the grounds. The *Saladin* of Gloucester was a typical vessel of that period when sail-driven clipper craft were being converted to auxiliary by installation of gasoline motors. A Globe engine of 100 horsepower was installed in the *Saladin*, in service with the fleet during 1909.

145. The seining fleet at rest, Louisburg, C.B. Driven to harbor by dense fog that persisted for days, the seining fleet numbering nearly seventy sail came to rest in the historic harbor at Louisburg, Cape Breton, awaiting favorable conditions to proceed. The photo was taken in June, 1910.

146. Nightfall. Louisburg. Darkness will soon prevail over the quiet harbor, and the lights of the seining fleet, swinging at anchor, shall gleam like stars through the night.

147. Splicing a new purse line. Discarding the purse line that seemed a bit tender, the bos'n, whose duty it is to keep rigging and gear in order, splices a new one of Russian hemp.

148. Overhauling the gear. While seiners are at anchor, there's always plenty to do. Here we see the crew breaking out salt barrels and overhauling the rigging, preparatory to leaving port when the fog clears away.

149. Seiners working on a school. The school settled away, but eagle-eyed mastheadmen spotted them and five seiners are hovering around where they were last seen, hoping for a "set." Note the men at the masthead, and schooner *Pinta's* seineboat towing from the port boom alongside.

150. Seiner *Clintonia*, cruising on the grounds. Many fine vessels were engaged in the mackerel fishery and schooner *Clintonia*, of Gloucester, was one of the representative craft of her day.

151. The seining fleet. On every hand, as far as the eye could see, vessels of the seining fleet were cruising about, working on fish. Two of them have taken large schools, their headsails doused, showing they have what the fishermen call "a jib haul."

152. A brush to windward. Rare occasion this, for Al Miller, one of the best helmsmen out of Gloucester, skipper of the *Indiana*, works up on the weather quarter of the *Elmer Gray*, of Boston, with none other than the mackerel king, Sol Jacobs, at the wheel. A friendly brush offshore, just to stretch their wings.

153. Seiner, picking up the boat. Having taken a school and finished pursing the seine, the seineboat is ready for the vessel to come alongside to bail.

154. Making passage. There's little room to spare aboard a seiner and when making passage to or from Gloucester the decks are well taken up with seineboats, dories, seines, and gear stowed in every available space.

155. Nearing the grounds. Approaching the cruising grounds where mackerel may be expected, mastheadmen aloft note every indication fish are in the vicinity. Flocks of sea geese hovering over the water are eagerly watched, and at night movements of small pods of herring, kyacks, and bluebacks are scrutinized from aloft to determine whether they are driven by schools of mackerel. Their presence is almost a certain sign mackerel are there. At once they are sighted, the seineboat is cleared away and preparations made to launch the boat and "make on" the seine, ready for a set.

156. Launching the seineboat. Seineboats are heavy, and care must be exer-
cised launching them over the side to prevent damage to the boats and injury
to crew. As the vessel rolls to and fro in the ground swell, the boat must be
kept clear of rigging and rail as the tackles are slacked away. Once afloat,
the boat boom is swung out and the seineboat painter eased off to bring the
boat alongside just aft the main rigging, opposite the seine roller.

. "Making on" the seine.
re we see the big seine
ng over the roller into
seineboat alongside,
seineheaver and bight
ser stowing it neatly in
ls just aft the thwarts
the oarsmen.

. Ready for business.
e seineboat splashes
rrily alongside as the
sel proceeds, the seine
l all the gear ready and
place the moment re-
red. The skipper's steer-
oar rests on the seine,
s handy, pump rigged,
ser uncovered, and
rything set.

. "Get in the boat!"
hting a school almost
d ahead, just to port, the
kout aloft starts some-
g and the skipper takes
the rigging to "have a
k." One glance tells him
fish are mackerel and
school "ringing," as they
m it when the fish re-
in in one spot and swim
und in a circle. "Get in
boat!" he roars, and
an instant comes slid-
down the rigging and
bles in after them.

160. The seineboat in action, after the school. With eyes glued to the spot where mackerel were sighted, the skipper takes his post atop the seine in the after part of the boat, and with a hasty order to the helmsman they are off, full speed.

161. "Drive her, boys, drive her!" With long and powerful strokes the rugged fishermen bend their oars as they buckle down to it and drive the seineboat speeding toward the distant school. With rhythmic swing the oars go, to and fro, the skipper urging them on, shouting, "Drive her, boys, drive her!"

162. The seineboat gets a "set." Having circled the school of mackerel successfully, both ends of the great seine are now aboard the seineboat and the crew begin to purse up, or "dry in" the twine, until the imprisoned fish are herded together in the smallest possible area. The corks keep the top of the seine at the surface.

163. They get the school. Picking up the boat. The seine "dried in," the boat crew hang on the twine holding the fish and signal the vessel to pick them up. Not so easy to shoot the craft alongside with just sufficient headway, and secure the boat in position to bail fish without straining the twine. The tremendous weight, perhaps hundreds of barrels of imprisoned mackerel, might burst the seine if too sudden strain be brought upon it.

164. Seineboat alongside, ready to bail. Bracing their oars against the vessel, two of the crew keep the seineboat clear so bailing may proceed, leaving plenty of room for the skipper to dip the long-handled scoop net, holding five or six barrels at each dip.

165. Up comes the scoop net. Down goes the net, and up it comes with wriggling mackerel.

166. A close-up of the scoop net. The husky seineheaver looks with evident satisfaction at the dripping net as it emerges, half-filled with fine mackerel of largest size, plump and hard.

167. The bailing crew, hard at it. The skipper, at the right, wields the handle of the scoop net; two men stationed at the rail grasp the scoop and dump the fish on deck; and the hoisting gang, two of whom are seen at the left, are stationed amidships. Nowadays the hoisting is done with power winches.

168. Up over the rail comes the net. This school had plenty of herring and hickory shad mixed in, and the scales fly in all directions as they hit the deck.

169. Dumping 'em out. Already well-surrounded, the men stationed at the rail dumping the net will soon be waist-high in mackerel, and by nightfall the vessel's deck filled from stem to stern.

170. Bailing a jib haul. Both headsails doused, to ease the vessel as she lays with a tremendous haul of mackerel alongside. Twenty thousand fish were iced below decks and the remainder salted until every barrel aboard was filled and all the salt wet.

171. The decks, filled rail to rail, with fine, fat mackerel.

172. Joining the fleet. With seineboats on deck and plenty of salt below, this big twiner fresh from Gloucester has been driving eastward to join the Cape Shore fleet before the mackerel schools pass by. Down comes the balloon and sheets are eased off as she shoots alongside to get the news, for we are dressing mackerel.

173. Toilers of the sea. Decks heaped rail high with mackerel to split for salting, the crew toil day and night, and 5 A. M. shows them still at it.

174. When daylight came. Splitting and gibbing mackerel all through the night, daylight finds the crew still dressing fish and the decks crowded with barrels, with hardly room for the splitting gangs to work. These, called wash barrels, must all be repacked and salted later, before the fish are finally in prime condition and the barrels coopered.

175. Homeward bound to Gloucester with a full hold. The vessel, half-sunk with mackerel, every barrel filled, coopered, and no worries about securing a fare, the skipper begins to worry about the price he'll get when he arrives to sell the trip.

176. Back to Gloucester again. The trip sold and fish discharged at the market, the vessels haul into the dock to overhaul gear and refit, taking aboard ice and provisions, ready to sail again.

177. Laying up for winter. At the close of the seining season, late in the fall, the mackerel vessels, greyhounds of the fishing fleet, were usually laid up during the winter months. Gear was removed and stowed away in the warehouses ashore; fresh paint as a reward for faithful service might be forthcoming, and the deserted craft left to themselves, alone and forgotten, until spring.

178. Mending nets.

179. Mackerel seiners resting during the winter. Formerly vessels engaged in the mackerel fishery were laid up to rest during the winter months at Gloucester, leaving the haddockers and halibut fleet to carry on during the strenuous season of winter fishing on the eastern banks and Georges.

180. Setting the gill nets.

181. Gill netting for mackerel. Having hauled his nets at daylight, the fisherman returns alongside and is passing the mackerel aboard in baskets. During the night the nets are located by lanterns spaced every ten nets apart, erected on floats, which may be seen on the stack of nets in the dory.

182. An unwelcome catch. While underrunning mackerel gill nets, the fisherman discovered one completely wrapped around an enormous shark which, having gorged himself liberally on the enmeshed mackerel, found himself snarled in the twine. After thrashing around until the net became so tight further struggle was impossible, he gave up the battle and was towed alongside the vessel where the skipper finished him off with an ax. The wooden floats near the stern of the dory are attached to the top of the net.

183. Monster mackerel shark. Sharks and dogfish are the enemy of the mackerel fisherman, doing great damage to the expensive seines and nets. Tearing great gaps in the tarry twine, mackerel thus liberated escape and cause great financial losses. This enormous shark, 14 feet in length, became ensnared in one of the gill nets astern of schooner *Massasoit*, and became so tightly tangled in the twine it was dead when hoisted aboard. The photo was taken in 1905.

184. The *Lois Corkum*, type of auxiliary seiner that followed the Gloucester sailing vessels.

185. Small type vessels seining, 1939. The fleet of big vessels formerly engaged in mackerel seining has practically disappeared, but few remaining of a fleet once numbering hundreds. Smaller craft have taken their places, power driven; and the larger seiners now in service are practically all converted from the fleet of 110-foot submarine chasers built during the World War, driven by Diesel engines.

186. Sub chasers converted into mackerel fleet, 1940.

5. *Cod, Haddock, and Halibut*

187. The water front at Gloucester. The wharves and water front of Gloucester yielded a wealth of material for artists, and although the march of time has wrought many changes, the beautiful etchings and paintings by famous artists have preserved its charm for all time.

188. Cod nets drying out at Gloucester. Nets were often set for cod in certain spots of sheltered coastal waters, as in Ipswich Bay, and the drying reels set up along the wharves were always a source of interest and attraction.

189. Mending the twine. Cod nets, like all filmy, delicately woven material, although of unusual strength, frequently became damaged and torn, requiring care to maintain them in order. The fishermen are wonderfully clever with the shuttle and work patiently to keep the gear in good condition.

190. A sixteen-dory handliner. A bank of sixteen dories aboard a handliner is seldom seen today. The *J. M. Marshall* of Gloucester, aboard which this photo was taken, was engaged in fishing off the New England coast.

191. *Columbia* puts to sea. Schooner *Columbia*, pride of Gloucester, passes the whistler off Eastern Point under bank sail on her first trip salt fishing, bound for the Grand Banks.

192. A big knockabout trawler bound for the bank.

193. Working clear, T Wharf, Boston. On market days the haddockers were often three or four abreast along both sides of T Wharf, and it took close figuring sometimes to pull out. The big trawlers in the foreground have locked horns, their tremendous main booms overlapped and no room to swing clear.

194. Cutting up bait and baiting trawls on the bank.

195. Decks of a market trawler. There is little room to spare aboard a trawler on deck, but when the dories are out these trawl tubs will be in service filled with baited trawls, and the decks are clear until the fishermen come alongside and fork the fish aboard over the rail. This was a ten-dory craft, market fishing and operating from T Wharf at Boston.

196. A good day on the bank and the pens are filled with cod and haddock.

197. February on Georges.

198. Sighting a lost dory. Gone astray during a dense fog that swept down without warning, a missing dory is sighted the following day by the lookouts at the masthead. The hardy skipper takes the wheel himself to follow directions from aloft. With every nerve alert, his eye eagerly searches the horizon.

199. Haddockers in port, Gloucester.

200. Landing cod at the docks at East Gloucester.

201. Discharging fresh haddock. This trip of haddock from offshore will go to the splitters and pass on to the smokehouses for curing, to emerge later as finnan haddie for your Sunday morning breakfast.

202. Landing cod for the splitters.

203. Sorting out the cod. As the cod are hoisted ashore in baskets, fish of varying size are culled out and forked into heaps conveniently near the gangs of splitters.

204. Rinsing cod after splitting operations. After splitting, the cod are thoroughly rinsed and scrubbed preparatory to salting. Here we see men scrubbing fish in a dory filled with fresh, clean water.

205. Splitters at work, splitting and backboning the cod.

206. Ready to salt the cod. After rinsing in sea water, the cod are wheeled to the salting butts and salted down, layer upon layer, and the filled butts heaped up with salt on top as the fish settle considerably during the pickling process.

207. Packing cod in the salt butts. After rinsing, the cod are sprinkled with salt and carefully packed away in the salt butts for pickling. Packed flesh side up, a layer of fish, and a layer of salt. Here they will remain from one to two weeks before being kenched in stacks to press out the pickle preparatory to curing in the sun.

208. Inside the salt warehouse. Many thousands of cod are packed away pickling in these salt butts, the largest warehouse of its kind. Hundreds of great casks, filled to the brim with selected cod, carefully salted down and heavily covered with pure sea salt, white as snow.

209. Discharging salt at Gloucester. The salt used for curing salt cod at Gloucester came from the finest supply sources available: Trepani, Cádiz, and Turks Islands, brought thousands of miles across the sea. This vessel, the *Nostra Senora Assunta,* of Genoa, brought a cargo from Trepani in the Mediterranean Sea, and we see her discharging at East Gloucester at the warehouses, close by the curing flakes.

210. "Kenched" to press out the pickle. When thoroughly pickled, the cod are taken from the salt butts and put through a process called "water hawsing," to remove superfluous pickle. This consists of stacking them in heaps—or kenching, the fishermen call it—to press out the pickle not absorbed by the fish.

211. Salt cod drying on the flakes at East Gloucester.

212. Salt cod curing in the sun. After thorough kenching, the cod are spread out to dry in fresh air and sunlight, the fish wheeled to the light wooden framework, called flakes, and spread flesh side up in clear, sunny weather to dry out.

213. Weighing off a trip of salt cod from the banks, at Gloucester.

214. Salt cod, cured, ready for market. The foreman of this producing plant has been in charge of curing and salting cod for many years, and exhibits a perfectly cured cod of unusual size and weight. In this condition, the fish is ready for sale, or may go to the skinners to be cut into fillets and boned, wrapped in cellophane, and packed for the fine trade as boneless salt cod.

215 and 216. Discharging a trip of fresh halibut caught in the deep, icy waters of the North Atlantic. This variety is called eastern halibut to distinguish it from that shipped from the Pacific coast. Its scarcity and the gradual disappearance of the halibut fleet make such a scene as this a rare occurrence today. Years ago the wharves at the Atlantic and American Halibut Company were busy discharging such trips of fresh or flitched halibut frequently. The giant halibut, two or three at a time, were hoisted out and swung into the warehouse scales to weigh off the trip. The photos show halibuter *Tacoma* discharging. Note the great cable, coiled amidships.

217. A quiet day in port.

218. Typical flounder dragger, 1928. Craft of this type built at the Maine shipyards were about 85 feet in length, equipped with engines of approximately 170 horsepower.

219. Flounder draggers, New Bedford. Sail-driven fishing schooners were fast disappearing about 1930, most of the surviving ones being converted to auxiliaries. Craft building for flounder dragging, cod and haddock fishing on Georges were of the type illustrated, power driven and seldom swinging anything more than a riding sail on the main.

220. Fresh from the builders. The first arrival at her home port after the run down the coast from Maine, this dragger arrives bedecked with colors fore and aft, pausing to be admired by a group of critical fishermen.

221. *Minnie V.*, dragger of the smaller type, fitted for scalloping.

222. Dragger *Mary R. Mullins* of New Bedford.

223. Dragger. *The Friars*, New Bedford.

224. Installing a Diesel engine aboard a dragger. Draggers require rugged gear and must be heavily powered to drag trawl nets and gates astern along the bottom against the wind, especially in heavy weather. This Diesel engine weighed fifteen tons, rated at 230 horsepower, and was installed aboard the New Bedford dragger *Noreen*, a 99-foot vessel, in 1936.

225. Powerful winches for hauling the trawl. The reeling or winding drums of the winches used aboard draggers of 90 to 100 feet in length have a capacity of about 360 fathoms of wire cable. They must be strongly built to take the strain, and the one here photographed aboard dragger *Julia & Eleanor* gives an adequate idea of how powerfully they are built.

226. Commissioned in spring 1940, the 112-foot dragger *St.-George* represents the last word in development of the New England-built wooden fishermen. Designed by Albert E. Condon, Thomaston, Maine, built by Snow Shipyards, Inc., at Rockland, Maine, under American Bureau of Shipping supervision, she has a capacity for 180,000 lbs. iced fish between watertight bulkheads, and is equipped with every modern device for safety and efficiency. The power plant is a 500 horsepower direct reversing Fairbanks-Morse engine, driving 5½ inch bronze shaft. Her rating, class AIE, is the same as that given modern steel trawlers.

227. Scallopers and draggers at Fairhaven. A large fleet of deep-sea scallopers operates from New Bedford, their distinguishing mark being two swinging booms for handling scallop drags.

228. Tending the Sakonnet anchor trap. Operating from Newport, the steam fisherman *Vigilant* here engages in hauling the daily catch.

229. The *Sea Ranger* returns from Georges in winter. Looking aft.

230. The *Sea Ranger* returns from Georges in winter. Looking forward.

231. The *Four Sisters*. An American Billingsgate. Caught on the Bank in the path of the mid-September hurricane, 1940, the deep-sea scallop fleet and draggers scampered back to port for shelter. For two days they poured into New Bedford harbor until the fish piers were crowded and vessels were huddled together across the pier heads in friendly groups along the entire water front. The four vessels abreast in the foreground are deep-sea scallopers, and their V scallop booms may be plainly seen, swung inboard.

6. *Swordfishing off Nantucket*

232. Evening off Nantucket.

233. Fitting out for the swordfishing season. Schooner *Hazel M. Jackson* of Edgartown, Mass., built at Thomaston, Maine, in 1920, was for years high line among the swordfishing fleet on the New England coast.

234. The swordfishing "pulpit" on the bowsprit. The bosn's seat slung from the iron body brace placed at the outer end of the bowsprit completes the arrangement for convenience and steadying of the striker while cruising on the grounds.

235. Almost ready to go, taking the ice. Swordfish are in season off the New England coast in midsummer, when fog and hot weather are prevalent, and tons of ice are taken aboard to preserve the fish and assure their perfect condition upon arrival in port.

236. Swordfisherman cruising on the grounds. All hands are alert once the swordfish feeding grounds are reached, and here we see the masthead lookout aloft eagerly scanning the sunlit sea, watching for the fin of a swordfish unsuspecting as he swims about in search of food. The striker is at his post by the pulpit, harpoon handy, ready for business.

237. "Swordfish to port!" The wary swordfish does not always "fin" on the surface, but frequently swims crazily about several feet below, zigzagging first one way and then another. The lookout has spotted one and plotted his course to place the fish between the vessel and the sun so its movements may be followed, and all hands but the helmsman hasten aloft to aid the mastheadman.

238. "Fish dead ahead, steady!" Through skillful maneuvering the helmsman has placed the vessel in a position where the shadow of the fish can be seen plainly, dead ahead, and close aboard. So close aboard that the skipper takes no chances of losing the strike and slides down the headstay to the pulpit, ready to plunge the iron into the fish if within reach.

239. Striking a swordfish. Striking, or ironing a swordfish, as the fishermen call it, is a difficult operation when the fish is swimming deep beneath the surface. Sensing danger from the shadow of the approaching vessel, the fish darts away hastily and it requires quick work and a steady hand to make the strike. The skipper ironed this fish perfectly as it dove away, pitchpoling the harpoon.

240. A difficult strike. The skipper backboned this fish and drove the iron clear through, just before it got beyond reach. During the cruise at the time this photo was taken the skipper had forty-four chances on fish, and ironed all but one.

241. Over goes the keg. Once the swordfish is ironed, the line attached to the harpoon barb is slacked away and cast overboard as the fish darts away at full speed. The end of the forty-fathom line is bent on the keg which we see being dropped over to clear the propeller. The keg acts as a drag and marker as well, for movements of the fish can be readily seen from aboard.

242. Away goes the swordfish. Often when first struck the fish swims away at a swift pace, towing the telltale keg astern. The fishermen keep clear and allow the swordfish plenty of time to weaken before they make any attempt to haul it toward the surface.

243. Over goes the dory, ready to haul. In the foreground may be seen the line, coiled on deck, ready for another fish, and the keg attached.

244. Picking up the keg. The stationary keg floating peacefully on the surface looks innocent enough, but the skipper eyes it suspiciously as he prepares to cast off the doryman. The half-drowned-out fish may be sulking below, ready to fight the instant he feels the strain on the line as the doryman cautiously takes in the slack.

245. Feeling out the fish. The doryman has taken the keg aboard and gingerly feels the movements of the swordfish as the line is slowly taken in, for the fish may still be strong and full of fight, making a rush for the dory. This sometimes happens.

246. Doryman, ready to come aboard. After weakening the fish to such extent that it may be safely hauled to the surface and lanced in the gills, the fisherman secures it alongside the dory by taking a turn around the tail and signals the vessel to pick him up.

247. Hoisting the swordfish aboard. The dory alongside, the line around the fish's tail is passed aboard and the fish hauled into the cockpit. This is a small fish, weighing about 175 pounds when dressed.

248. Hauling a swordfish. While a swordfish backboned may give a few convulsive shivers and pass out peaceably and others dive below and sulk until practically drowned out, there are occasions when a long-drawn-out tussle for mastery ensues. This fish had no intentions of rising and fought for every fathom of line. The fisherman weighing 235 pounds requires all his weight and strength to hold the struggling fish and prevent the dory from being capsized. Darkness fell before the giant fish was taken aboard.

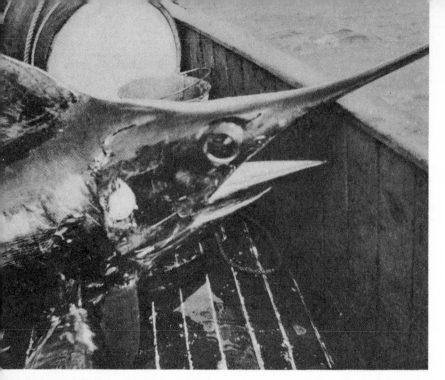

249. Mr. Swordfish poses for his portrait. Note the large eyes and absence of teeth in his mouth.

250. Coming aboard, still full of fight. This swordfish, a big fellow, appeared to be about done up when brought alongside, but developed considerable energy when hauled floundering into the cockpit.

251. The finishing touch. The swordfish's sword, his weapon of defense, is a menacing danger and must be removed at once. This fish was a husky brute and dressed nearly 500 pounds.

252. An afternoon catch. Three small fish and a 400-pounder taken late that afternoon made up for a fruitless search over the sea during the morning hours when the school refused to fin.

253. Hauling a fish from on board. On this occasion the skipper decided to haul the fish from the cockpit on board instead of trailing in the dory. Note the tension and anxious expression of the men as the fish nears the vessel.

254. Lancing the fish. Brought close to the surface and alongside, the fish gave the skipper a brief opportunity to jab the lance into its gills.

255. The final thrust. The exhausted swordfish, already hauled half-out of water, is kept head down as the skipper holds the lance deep into the gills until the fish can be taken aboard without danger from the sword.

256. Ironed through. This unusual view aboard the swordfisherman gives definite proof of the skipper's skill as striker, for the harpoon barb shows plainly under the throat where it was driven entirely through the fish, leaving no chance for the iron to draw while hauling.

257. Dressing and scrubbing the fish. Toward nightfall the crew dress and scrub the fish thoroughly, salt the nape and pack with cracked ice before the fish are stowed in the hold and buried in ice to keep them in prime condition.

258. Back in port to market the trip. Returned to port, the crew remove the fish from the ice pens below deck to prepare them for market.

259. Preparing the trip for sale. On deck, the swordfish are once more thoroughly scrubbed and the ice removed from the nape for inspection.

260. The catch goes to market. After inspection the swordfish are hoisted out and weighed at the wholesaler's, from where they are shipped to the retail trade throughout the country.

261. The old windlass, swordfisherman *Two Forty*, Portland.

Appendix

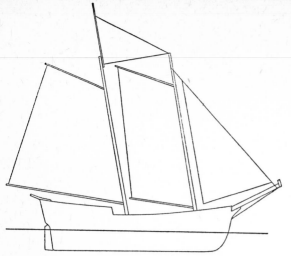

1. Early Grand Banker, "Heeltapper," 1741, about 65 feet.

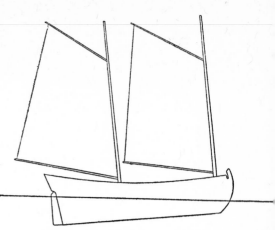

2. Chebacco boat, 1780–1800, about 34 feet.

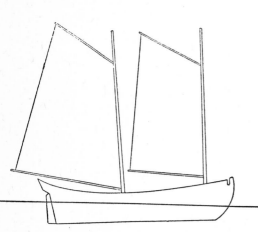

3. Dogbody, 1800–1810, about 36 feet.

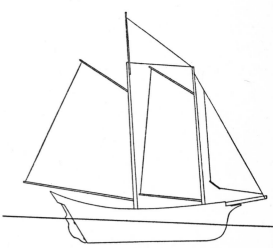

4. Pinkey, 1810–1830, about 48 feet.

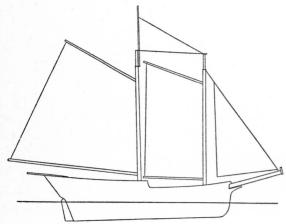

5. Low quarter-deck schooner, 1830, about 65 feet.

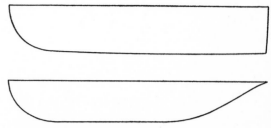

6. Halfbreadths of an early Grand Banker, "Heeltapper," 1741, and Pinkey, 1810–1830.

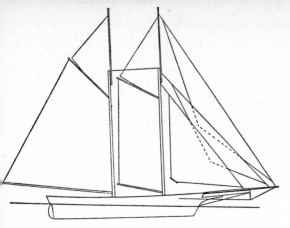

7. Clipper of 1870, 75 feet.

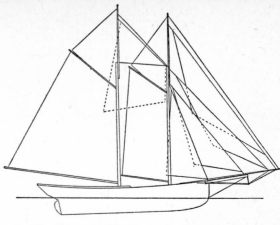

8. *Grampus,* 1885, first of the plumb stem schooners.

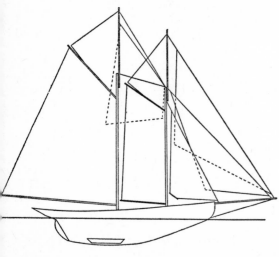

9. *Massasoit,* 1898, the first fisherman to carry outside ballast.

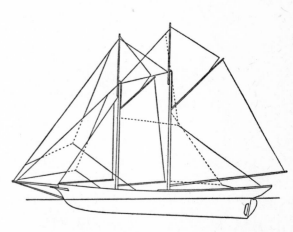

10. *Helen M. Gould,* 1900, the first 125-foot gasoline auxiliary.

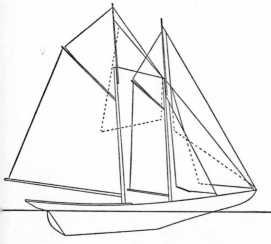

11. The first knockabout type of 1902—*Helen B. Thomas.*

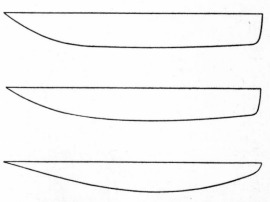

12. Halfbreadths of *Romp,* the first sharp-bowed craft, 1847; a mackerel clipper, 1880; *Massasoit,* 1898.

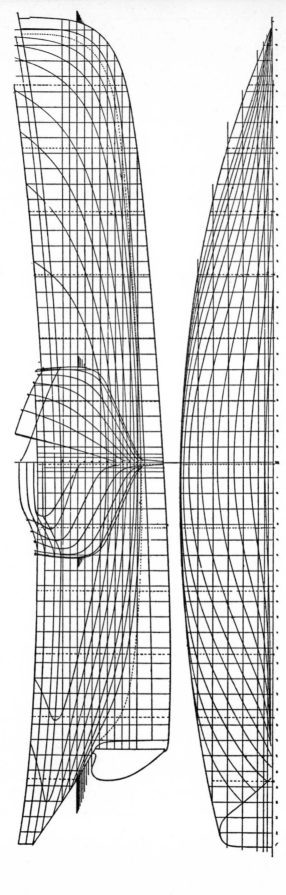

13. Lines of the famous fisherman *Harry Belden* (1889). Schooners *Susan R. Stone* and *Governor Russell* were built from the same plans, credited to Edward Burgess.

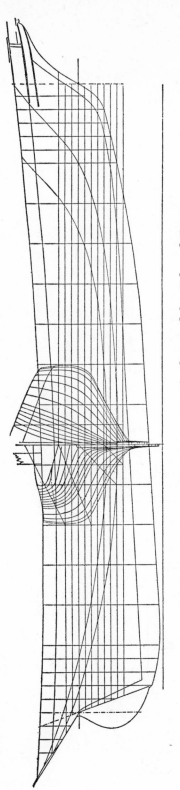

14. Lines of schooner *Fredonia* (1889), designed by Edward Burgess.

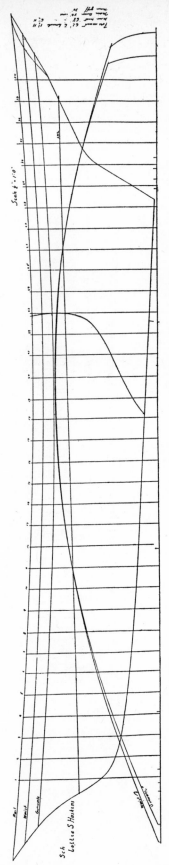

15. Lines of the fast fisherman *Lottie S. Haskins* (1890), taken from the original model made by George Mel. McClain.

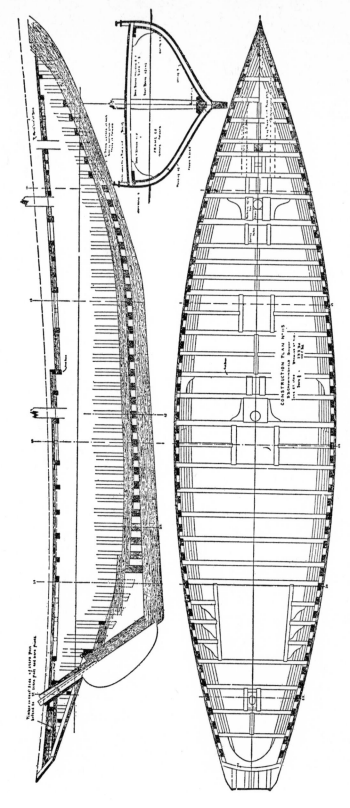

16. Construction plan, schooner *Rob Roy* (1900), designed by Crowninshield.

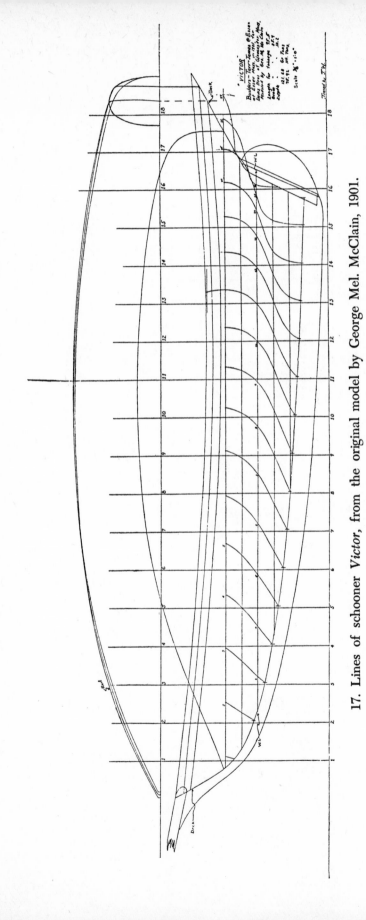

17. Lines of schooner *Victor*, from the original model by George Mel. McClain, 1901.

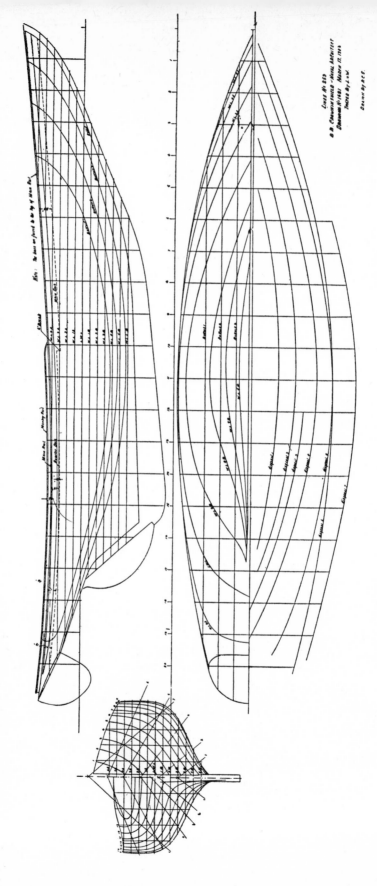

18. Lines of schooner *Stranger*, designed by B. B. Crowninshield, 1903.

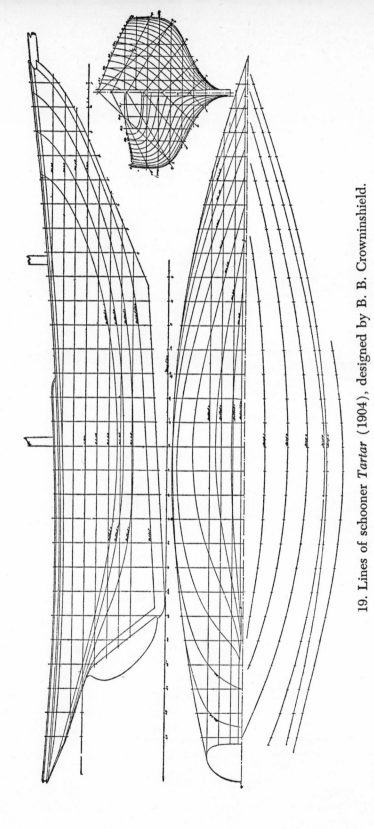

19. Lines of schooner *Tartar* (1904), designed by B. B. Crowninshield.

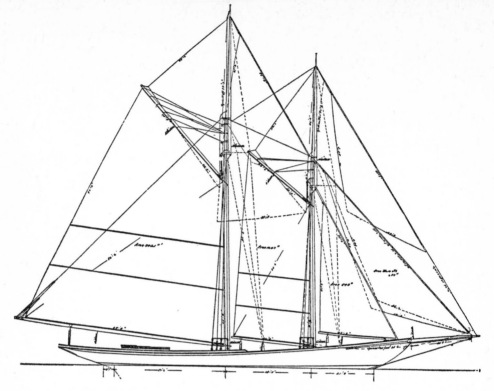

20. Sail plan, schooner *Tartar* (1904), by Crowninshield.

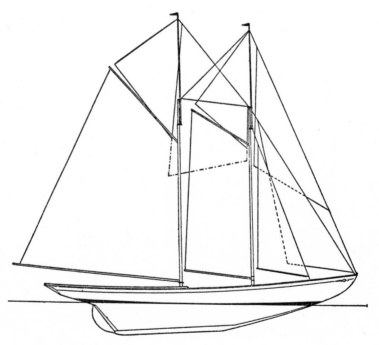

21. Typical sail plan, McManus fishing schooners, 1904.

Table of offsets for the schooner, rotated 90°. Column headings are the station numbers.

Stations.	Rabbe on Stem	2.	6.	10.	14.	18.	22.	26.	30.	34.	38.	42.	46.	Stem.
Height of Deck Sheer above Load Water Line.	2.9.4	7.7.6	6.8.4	5.10.4	5.1.3	4.5.5	3.11.6	3.7.6	3.6.0	3.4.3	3.6.1	3.10.0	4.2.3	4.7.2
" on Rail " Deck Sheer	2.0.0		2.0.0	1.10.4	2.0.0	2.0.0	2.0.0	2.0.0	2.0.0	2.0.0	2.0.0	1.10.6	1.9.4	1.8.6
" Rabbet on Keel + Base Line			11.9.4	2.9.6	7.11.2	7.0.5	6.4.7	5.10.1	5.6.0	5.0.7				
" Cotton of " " "		13.2.0	11.0.3	7.7.0	5.10.4	4.7.2	3.8.1	3.5.5	2.1.8	2.1.4				
Half Breadth, Rail Sheer		2.0.6	6.6.4	8.8.7	9.10.4	10.10.3	11.4.4	11.6.3	11.8.2	10.9.1	9.9.4	8.5.3	6.9.2	5.0.0
" " Deck		3.7.6	6.1.1	8.1.4	9.8.1	10.9.1	11.4.4	11.7.3	11.4.1	10.9.5	9.9.4	8.2.4	5.11.3	3.4.0
" " 2nd water line above load line		2.9.7	5.3.2	7.9.1	9.6.4	10.9.0	11.4.4	11.7.3	11.4.2	10.9.5	9.9.4	8.3.4	6.5.5	
" " 1st "		1.9.1	4.6.1	7.1.0	9.1.0	10.5.6	11.3.5	11.7.3	11.3.2	11.0.1	9.3.0	7.0.5	1.6.0	
" " Load water line			3.3.5	6.0.0	8.2.4	8.3.2	10.0.4	11.0.4	9.8.0	9.3.3	7.0.5			
" " 1st water line below load water line		1.4.4	4.1.3	6.5.4	7.3.0	7.1.2	9.7.4	9.1.0	7.1.0	2.1.7				
" " 2nd " "			1.6.0	3.9.0	5.3.1	6.5.6	6.7.5	5.6.3	2.1.0	0.11.1				
" " 3rd "		1.6.4		0.7.5	2.3.0	3.2.5	3.3.5	2.1.4	1.3.3	0.6.4				
" " 4th "						0.8.2	0.8.2	0.2.6	0.7.6	0.5.6				
" of Keel on rabbet line		0.4.0	0.4.4	0.5.0	0.5.5	0.6.0	0.6.0	0.6.0	0.6.0	5.4.0.0				
" " on Diagonal A.		3.3.2	5.4.1	8.2.1	10.6.0	11.7.6	12.2.1	12.3.3	11.4.6	9.10.0	7.8.0	5.1.0	3.3.0	
" " B.		9.7.1	5.0.2	7.2.0	8.1.1	10.3.0	11.2.1	10.9.1	10.9.4	9.8.4	7.0.3	5.3.4	2.2.3	
" " C.		1.6.4	8.1.4	5.9.0	7.4.0	8.5.6	9.1.4	2.2.3	2.8.1	7.5.3	5.7.2	2.9.4		

Section after body Two (2) feet out; Heights taken from base line.
Measurements taken in feet inches and eighths.
Stations spaced eight (8) feet apart, Water lines spaced Two (2) feet apart.
Base line situated (14) fourteen feet below load water line.
Position of Diagonals.
Diagonal A. on center line (20) twenty feet above base line & will load line 10 ft. out
Diagonal B. " " " (18) eighteen " " 5.11.6 "
Diagonal C. " " " (16) sixteen " " 9.7.0 "

Rabbet on stem from station #6 16.11.0. 16.4.3 12.0.0. 8.6.4 2.10.6
Stem moulded 9 in outside of rabbet
Rabbet on Post abaft Station #38 8.11.4 6.11.4 5.8.0. 4.5.0 3.24.
Back of " " " " 9.6.0. 7.11.4 6.10.4 5.9.4 4.8.4.
Round of Stem at rail 8 inches
function of Stem & rail to load line 9 ft. out at station #38 20.0.0
" " " " above load water line. 4.0.0
" " " Rail " " " abaft station #38 6.5.6.
" " " " abaft station #38 23.8.0

Table of Schooner for Capt. Crowell et al.
March 15th 1902.
Lines and Tables to be returned to
Thomas F. McManus
Boston Mass.

22. Table of offsets by designer Thomas F. McManus for laying down lines in the mold loft, full size, from which schooners *Flora S. Nickerson* and *Matchless* were built. In the old days builders worked from wooden models built up in sections which were taken apart when completed, and the necessary calculations were figured out from them. Reference to the table gives an idea of the great care and accuracy required of the designer in order that the vessel shall conform to his plans as nearly as possible.

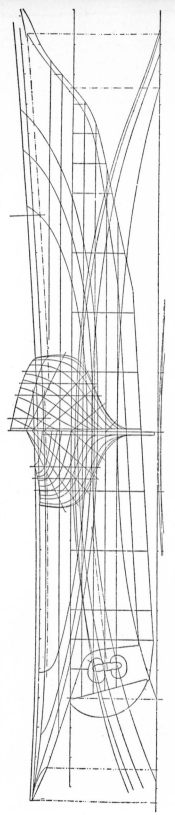

23. Lines of auxiliary schooner *Elizabeth Silsbee*, designed by W. Starling Burgess, 1905.

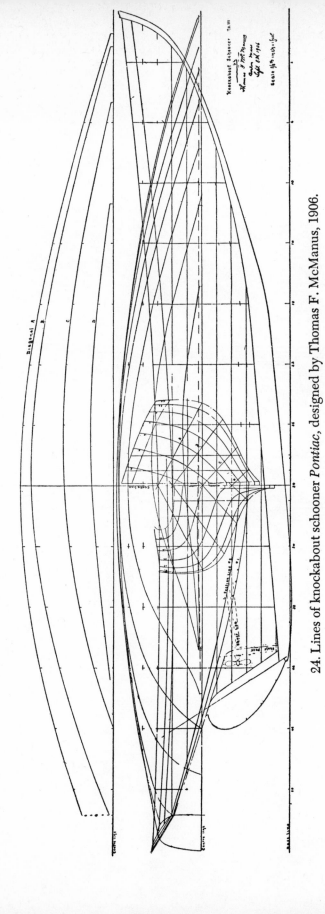

24. Lines of knockabout schooner *Pontiac*, designed by Thomas F. McManus, 1906.

SAIL PLAN
of
J.A.MATHESON'S.

Sch.

by
Thomas F. McManus. Des.

Boston Mass.
Sept. 1ˢᵗ 1909.
Scale ⅛ᵗʰ inch = 1 foot.

25. Sail plan, McManus knockabout schooner *Gladys & Nellie*, 1909.

190

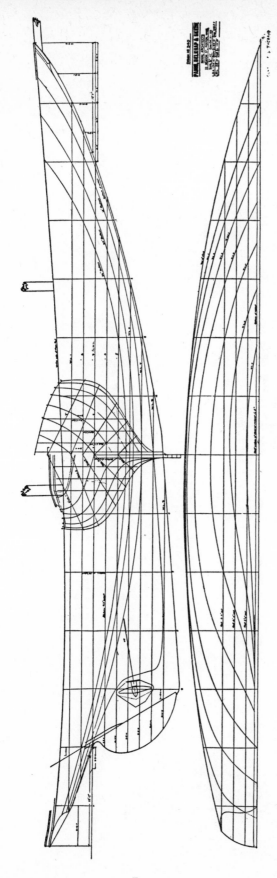

26. Lines of famous schooner *Gertrude L. Thebaud*, last of the great fleet of clipper fishermen that formerly hailed from Gloucester. Designed by Paine, Belknap & Skene in 1929, and published by the courtesy of Frank C. Paine of Boston.

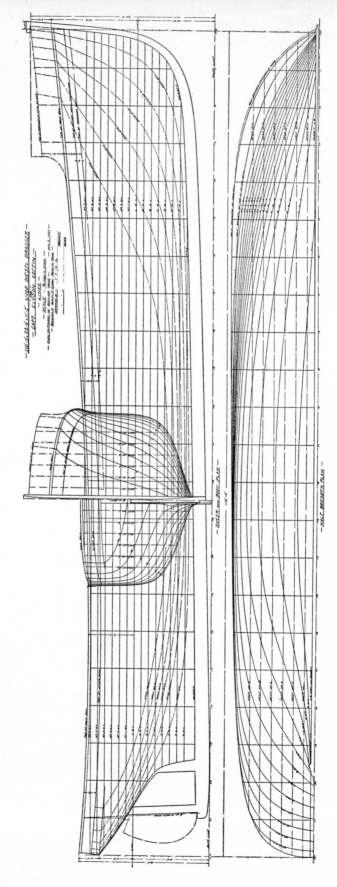

27. Lines of the 110-foot wooden hull Diesel dragger *St. George*, designed by Albert E. Condon, 1940.